ONLY THE
SENSES SLEEP

New Issues Poetry & Prose

Editor	Herbert Scott
Copy Editor	Curtis VanDonkelaar
Managing Editor	Marianne Swierenga
Assistant to the Editor	Kim Kolbe

New Issues Poetry & Prose
The College of Arts and Sciences
Western Michigan University
Kalamazoo, MI 49008

First Edition, 2006.

ISBN-10	1-930974-65-5 (paperbound)
ISBN-13	978-1-930974-65-4 (paperbound)

Library of Congress Cataloging-in-Publication Data:
Miller, Wayne
Only the Senses Sleep/Wayne Miller
Library of Congress Control Number: 2006924618

Art Director	Tricia Hennessy
Designer	Rebecca Eley
Production Manager	Paul Sizer
	The Design Center, School of Art
	College of Fine Arts
	Western Michigan University

ONLY THE
SENSES SLEEP

WAYNE MILLER

New Issues

WESTERN MICHIGAN UNIVERSITY

This book is for Jeanne, though I didn't know it when I started—

Contents

ONE

TWO

THREE

Acknowledgments

Thanks to the editors of the following publications, where these poems first appeared, sometimes in earlier versions:

American Literary Review: "Trakl the Pharmacist"

Boulevard: "All the Ghosts Are Blind," "Dear Sappho, [In the vast history between us]"

Center: "Suspension Triptych"

Chelsea: "Ukrainian Egg"

Crazyhorse: "My Apartment As a Diorama," "From the Porch"

The Gettysburg Review: "Ice Storm"

Interim: "Dear Sappho, [I know my body's a placeholder for light]"

LIT: "Crime Scene," "The Undressing"

Lyric: "Brodsky Smoking," "November Wind," "Sunset Study"

Notre Dame Review: "Empty Warehouse"

Painted Bride Quarterly: "A Year in the Present Tense"

The Paris Review: "Two Stieglitz Photographs," "The Poem in Which We're Stieglitz and O'Keeffe," "Reading Sonnevi on a Tuesday Night"

Poetry: "For the 20th Century," "Four Atget Photographs," "Sunrise Study," "Pollock" (as "In a Fall in a World of Fall"), "Night Stop, South of Lyon," "After Machado" (as "Siesta")

Quarterly West: "Cohesion Triptych," "Dear Sappho, [Everything's always in focus at once,]"

Sycamore Review: "Double Aubade," "Elegy," "Self-Portrait in a Blank Room"

The Texas Review: "Preservation Triptych"

Western Humanities Review: "Vermont" (as "Driving through Vermont"), "Rounding the Corner into 'Early Sunday Morning'" (as "Rounding the Corner into Hopper's 'Early Sunday Morning'")

"Sunrise Study" was reprinted on the Poetry Daily website (<<http://www.poems.com>>) on September 3, 2001.

"Dear Sappho, [In the vast history between us]" received the Lucille Medwick Memorial Award from the Poetry Society of America. Thanks to Maury Medwick, Terrence Hayes, and the PSA.

Much of this book was written with the support of a Ruth Lilly Fellowship from the Poetry Foundation and a C. Glenn Cambor Fellowship from Inprint, Inc. Thanks to both organizations. Thanks also to Ms. Ruth Lilly and Ms. Dana Hokin.

Thanks to Central Missouri State University, the University of Houston, and Writers in the Schools for their support—and for employing me.

Thanks to my writing teachers, especially Stuart Friebert, David Young, Martha Collins, Robert Phillips, Adam Zagajewski and Edward Hirsch.

Thanks to those who in various and important ways made this book possible: Tip Rushing, Hughes Sparks, Matt Hayden, Aaron Page, Jamie Rauer, John Koethe, Frank Ruy, Schantie Mahalaha, Julie Chor, Chris Santiago, Elizabeth Antalek, Tommy Kriegsmann, Susanne Bines, the DANY Appeals Bureau, Brian Barker, Murray Farish, Mark McKee, Pablo Peschiera, Miah Arnold, Julie Chisholm, Mike Theune, Sean Hill, Alissa Valles, Young Smith, Greg Oaks, Kathy Garlick, j. Kastely, Steve Liparulo, Eric Miles Williamson, Kevin Prufer, Claire Hero, Alan Michael Parker, Rick Barot, Mom and Dad. And, of course, Jeanne.

. . . nothing can be more abstract and unreal that what we actually see.
—Giorgio Morandi

. . . since / our knowledge is historical, flowing, and flown.
—Elizabeth Bishop

ONE

Self-Portrait in a Blank Room

This pictureless room feels submerged,
as if I'm living at the bottom of a diving well.
There are still nails left over from the last tenant,

so I can imagine the old look of things, though
there's nothing here of context. The walls
are merely screens for the window-light—

for the wash of passing cars, for the streetlamps
flicking on their false daytime as the steps
of night-walkers hit the room's white net.

I was here as a boy beside my mother's bed
while she lay at the bottom of her silent boat—
listing in the roll of her breath—the blank

unsayable between us like a hospital curtain.
I was here in my father's house, up late
with the glazed T.V. and the falling snow,

his bottles broken and emptied like words
in the kitchen sink. I was here at Frank's party—
the music changing shades, the conversation

turning above me like a parachute—sitting
in the empty chair I was offered upon arrival.
I was here in my hotel room in Mississippi,

having hung up with Susanne and the New
York traffic below her window. I was here
each time a book opened in my hands

and my then-obsession dumped meaning
through a trap door in the page. I was here
lying awake beside the rhythm of your breath,

shamelessly redrawing you in my mind
as a different person. When I left you,
the air hung between us like a raveling fabric,

the expanse of our yard trailing me
the whole drive. I lied to you often—to every
person I've loved—to keep myself held,

though these tapestries I wove from water
have burst their seals and drained to the floor.
I sleep in the quarters of the ghosts inside me—

meaning I'm planted in my body. I remember
driving green-yellow backroads in northern Ohio—
the cool spring air flushing the car's interior,

the barns alluring, *private property*, the cornfields
every now and then revealing a row. And there
was the rain's dull roof-glissando above

4th Avenue, where the coverless bed—no,
where everything held us in place by resisting us.
I knew this then, as I lay slipped fast inside you,

until the room changed key, until you rose
to wash, until my hands lost their spark.
What I'll allow myself to believe is admittedly

not much—the faint mirror of a blank wall,
the heart ringing with another's words
like the sympathetic vibration of a bell—.

The one who drinks his reflection from a bowl
of clear water, Bill Viola said—. Several hours ago,
at dusk, I watched my shadow fold inward

as the room rose to overtake it. My boundaries
seemed abandoned, and I joined the darkening
with the most beautiful of false belongings—

I believed the room couldn't remain without me.

Preservation Triptych

——Clotheshangers

Clavicles in his parents' closet,
those shepherd's crook faces
that replace our own. They hang
there in deep meditation

as he explores the empty clothes:
the lined pairs of shoes—
a historical progression—,
the mechanized tie rack

with its dangling blindfolds,
the box of pearls like pills
in the drawer of paired socks.
Standing by the line of sleeves,

he takes the wrist of an old blue shirt
and lifts it to his eye
like a floppy telescope,—
a deeper shade of darkness there,

the embalming smell of mothballs.
When he turns back to the lit bedroom,
he steps over a fallen hanger
lying tangled in its blouse.

————*Clothespins*

All those small (cheeping?) birds;
the old lady's still sleeping in the house.
Across the dunes, the ocean

sands his driftwood
in long somnolent strokes.
This dialogue between them—

their question-and-answer
a see-sawing of breaths.
Now the pins clasp the lines

like notes on a drooping staff—
a handwritten score of her memory.
When she wakes,

the sentences will come back to her,
the sentences hanging there
without the words.

——Buttons

The jar of buttons on his mother's vanity,
every size and shape,

like swollen grains of sand. Years
collected from the shirts of his family,—

stored there like washed-out faces
in a shoebox of photographs.

In an old picture, his great-grandmother
posed in a straightback chair,

thimble-thumbed, pressing a needle
through a piece of cloth.

His grandpa's standing beside her,
just a boy—. And now

he's snoring on the couch,
little coins on the shut eyes of his collar.

Reading Sonnevi on a Tuesday Night

A film of mist clings to the storm windows
as the thunder gets pocketed and carried away
in the rain's dark overcoat. A good reading night—

car wheels amplified by the flooded street,
leaf-clogged gutters bailing steadily, constant
motion beyond my walls echoing

my body's gyroscopic stillness. Sonnevi says
Only if I touch do I dare let myself be touched,
and that familiar and somewhat terrifying curtain

of reading slips around me, pinning sound
to the room's lost corners, pinning the room
to an emptying sky. I'm in the glacial grooves

of Sonnevi's words as he makes love
and listens to Mozart in a spare apartment,
now reawakens to her voice saying goodnight

so much that I couldn't sleep I was elated.
His world slips through the waterfall
of language and hovers here, on the other side,

in my apartment, where we listened to Monk
showering with the door open, soft-boiled eggs
by the pink light of the Chinese take-out,

made love against the footsteps of morning
commuters, smoked cigarettes on the fire escape
right up to the minute you left. Here,

we are in this continuousness—our lives
dissolved in the channels of written lines—
every word I've read was in me before I read it.

They're pulled from me like seconds
from the cistern of an unfinished life. Love's
endless weathering moves the body

of our words: we read to understand
we're not alone in it—*we carry one another,*
assuredly—

                though we do this alone.

A Year in the Present Tense

1. Summer

Walking across a golf course at night,
I stop to pick up a tee—
a thin funnel planted in the grass,

or perhaps the smallest ear horn ever made.
There are teenagers laughing
on the seventh green,

and there's the silence last year
when I stumbled onto a couple making love
in the cupped hand

of a sandtrap. (*Don't step on my glasses*
was all the girl said
as I hurried past their scattered clothes.)

From this slight rise, I can see
the arcs of the sprinklers sputter around
on a flat stretch of greens,

then collapse at the tap of a timer—

2. Fall on Prospect St.

A flattened paper bag
among the leaves in the gutter;

the road is held together
by seams of tar.

Children at Play, silhouettes
on yellow, cars

moving so slowly
you can walk with them.

Mrs. Anderson comes out
to light her Jack-O-Lantern,

her wrap-around porch
like an empty stage.

I wave across our yards,
leaves falling between us,

as Mr. Finke drags another
tarpful to the curb,

a long shadow
chasing his footsteps.

3. Christmas Eve

Light-sketched house frames
and Rorschach trees,
the sidewalks lined

with candlelit paper bags.
The town's soft light
like a penlight through a bedsheet,

the Presbyterian bell choir
ringing muffled glass notes—.
Below my window,

a bag has caught fire,
its bare candle
burning against the falling snow

as my parents wrap presents
twenty years ago,—
tinkling ornaments,

our old dog lapping
at the green preserving water.
The breath inside each glass ball

remains the same breath,
sealed the year I was born.
When the street fills

with the organ's voice
I'll hear our neighbors
finding their cars covered in snow.

4. Spring

And who is squeezing the soundless
accordion of your lungs?

Sunlight enters the room
through the ribs of the Venetian blinds.

The striped square
sits at the end of the bed like a child

we haven't had, escaped
to our room from her nightmares.

She slips into the space between us,
then climbs the wall,

spreading as she dissolves.
I whisper in your ear, *Time to wake up,*

as the paperboy chucks his bundle
of headlines to the doorstep.

Dear Sappho,

In the vast history between us
so much has happened—the bones

of the dead kept turning
into hammers. And now I lift

myself into each day
as if into my body, go to work,

and then at night, my lit room
slips down into the glass.

The factories blow their smoke
up through the snow, the city

lifts our lights a little closer
to the sky. Long after you died,

Jim Dine narrowed his world
to a big fat heart—like a bomb

in a corner of the museum.
So much is in motion out there

beneath the page of dust
paling the television's screen!

Somewhere, folks are digging
a well, while elsewhere

the lit needles of gunshots
and fireflies—. I can assure you

that our lives keep fracturing
into notes, I can promise you

that a white fence without light
is like a sail without wind.

Please believe me: we haven't
forgotten you—we walk

on our syllables (these shadows
of footsteps), we land

deep in beauty at the expense
of ourselves. Like color,

the stars keep arriving
into their presence—arriving

from so long before you. Still,
we have nothing to give you.

Our world slips through you
like sand through the bones

of your fingers—sand
you lay dreaming on as a girl,

sand that today we melt
to fill windows.

Ukrainian Egg

> *Remembering is a form of forgetting.*
> —Milan Kundera

Forget the pattern books
and the feel of a blank eggshell—

something between paper and bone.
Forget the bowls of dye like churchlight,

and the lines of wax
sealing in the color that will remain.

Batik is the art of erasing
what you want to keep. Fine.

Forget what's preserved
is what was lost.

Forget the kitchen table,
something cooking

and a window view of the park.
Forget the symmetry

of lines from the center
and why it is (or once was) important.

Forget the thin layer of shellac,
and the emptying—

the yolk blown out in threads
on an axis of air.

Hold the weight
of your breath in your hand.

Two Stieglitz Photographs

1. Apples and Gable, Lake George

The apples are a charcoal gray,
though they manage to shine hard
in the late afternoon's sheer. Rain

glasses their dark amplitude
like light revealing its substance at last—
gathering its mass into droplets,

halfway to falling. All in all,
they possess so much perfection
and still the twigs are able to hold them—

this balancing: every object
lovingly pinched in the jaws of gravity.
And the seal of surfaces:

the apples' skins,
the opaque window, the house's side.
What Stieglitz must have known:

if he'd photographed them,
the cracked apples at his feet
would have revealed their inner light.

2. From the Window—"291"

Night has dropped its black gelatin
onto New York City—scattered aureoles
of windows. Snow

hems the rooftops—faint chalk lines
dividing the building-on-building,
the surfaces stacked toward me:

one blurred, indistinct structure.
Lights are embedded there
like dead cells, and a clothesline

across the alley is a string of syllables,
a conversation between neighbors.
Words that have been uttered,

mouthed or shouted, the same words
so often repeated—. In this thick
snow-mute silence, you can hear echoes

of people as they disappear
from these towers of our cohabitation,
from the light they're flooded with.

Sunrise Study

Beneath the dark a breastmilk blue.
Cobblestones like planted loaves of bread,

blank warehouse walls cradling from sight
the machines of another century.

Silence coasts the bricks like music
trailing the silence of the boot-like steps
that homebound walker wears. Of course,

pain is what pain does—outside-the-window's
a hand forever in mid-gesticulation.

At any one point in time, half the world's
rocking in the other half's shadow,

as we are now. Each soul's wrapped
in a name's slick membrane, each image
enters through the liquid coating our eyes.

Each moment's a bailed teaspoon of water.

Nonetheless, the city's deadbolts
wind and unwind the gears of our living watch,
the books open and close like valves.

My neighbors' breathing holds me
because it continues to move. Unwavering

light under the door like a sheet of paper—
thinning now, as the city's tesserae
take the day's first pale sips,

as the street presses its bell to the window,
as our shared water begins dividing
across our dream-cold bodies.

What remains for us has always been
what's arriving. We know this,

dearest belief—we know you each second,
only the senses sleep.

After Machado

The mugs in the kitchen
cradle their cupped air, the faucet
holds back its release of water,

though I can make out an occasional
wet stamp against the porcelain.

Out on the balcony, the leaves
tremble as the upstairs watering
silently threads down the vines;

in the street café, the plates lift
like flattened bells from the tables.

I'm learning to release
the world from the straps and float it
in the lit pools of its own surfaces.

I'm learning to lie here beside it,
to allow its breath against my neck:

the sunlight heating the room
in diminished half-tones. By four o'clock,
when I toss the topsheet aside,

the world will have put its hands
all over me, as it does every second—

sometimes less amicably. I'm learning
to yield to this intimacy—this press
of being against my body

can weigh the same as my eyelids.

November Wind

> Immured here
> by infinitely minute and endlessly exact details—.

Air ink-rolls the water, where far off
a trawler's anchored by a cloudlike net.

A curtain blows through a window,
gray (damp) along the bottom lace.

Cars in the street like hollowed cells,
their passengers naming certain stops

arrivals. To name these arrivals—
a ship, a curtain, a face—your soul trailing

like a net. The ice wind cuts through.
Yes, to speak it now, and thus absolve it

like a read word. Or else there's no wind,
just the whipping of your shirt.

TWO

For the 20th Century

1.
Now that it's dark, I can say
thank god my piece of you went down with the sun—
that ancient Christ-like ship—.

2.
Our past hums red
like a blood slide held up to the light,
a thin wash of cells. The body we keep opening
to spill its contents for a closer reading.
Days drift behind the blousy curtain . . . .

3.
Our years in a house with an all-sunset view—
we kept the shades drawn tight. Nothing to do
but rearrange the furniture
and play the boardgames for keeps.

4.
Why not brush on another layer of red?—
memory's erasure—the immuring scrim of all we know.
History's alchemy will explain away the big stuff,
while the interior of a life
cups its soul in its callused palm.

5.
When I wake before morning
I let the booklight fill the night silence—my room,
the tiny part of you I lived. Outside,
the stoplight keeps cycling over
in the held breath of its empty intersection.

6.
Each living cell numbered on the calendar—
blood in my body's sponge. Looking back,
I must admit I'll miss you.
I know you won't ask me to explain why.

Crime Scene

Beside the trashcans, beneath the window and the stoop,
lies the covered body. A pool of blood has spread
and dried, and now the cops have gathered
to focus their attention on this man

they could have passed obliviously yesterday.
One inspects the soles of his shoes, another
drops his glasses into a plastic bag. Two photographers
keep looking through their viewfinders,

while here in the audience, behind the tape,
we rattle around theories like ice in a tumbler—
wasn't from the neighborhood, must have been
a gang thing, etc. Whatever the story, this body's acquired

an almost impossible magnetism—we've considered
leaving since we got here, but the flashes
have yet to stop sputtering, and we can't entirely believe
that the sheet between us won't be removed.

All the Ghosts Are Blind,

                              —there's nothing
          in their eyes to catch the light.

          Stumbling through the chords
          of their routines, or hovering in corners

          lit by the penumbral glow
          of a television, waiting for the wakes

          of our passages to guide them.
          We lead them down hallways,

          through the stairwells and streets
          of the city, until we stop;

          they drift up to us like boats to a dock,
          nudging us with their faces,

          reaching for our words,
          which they cannot feel, but which

          fill them as water
          fills the air beneath the tap. And this

          blood of wind is all we have
          to give them, and they receive it

          obliviously—their body
          spilling through their absence.

Trakl the Pharmacist

Silence lives in empty windows, or in blue spaces,
or in gelatin. Lamplight: leaning over the table,
measuring slips of powder on a silver scale—

slivers of white to be capsuled. The pills shine
like a crowded constellation of opals, oblong bells
singing silently of the mouth's dark complaint.

The consoling solitude of fingerwork—
the mind numbed and slipped away to an icy blue.
Of course, pain is always waiting—time-joined

to these measurings in a back hospital room.
Each pill will dissolve word-like in a stranger's throat,
though for now they're perfect—fetally sealed

and still. They bear the poisons used to heal
the golden image of man—that unborn child—,
Trakl's breath hanging breathless inside them.

Brodsky Smoking

Later he'll write:
Because we go and beauty stays, though

now he's sitting listlessly at his desk
in the winter window-light of Venice,

his exhalations spreading into the room—
how the air sands off the light's edges

merely by touching one's lungs!
So perhaps I'll take him on a walk

in the damp cold, collar up,
passing along the cataracted water

and the sculpted walls of his seeing.
In the tunnel of both directions,

distance gathers the fog to opaque,
until the Grand Canal, where it opens

to chalk, where two faint boats like bells
ring each other with their wakes.

Standing on the Carità's steps,
he lights an MS with the hovering tear

of a match, inhales sharply—this symbol
of holding in the visible—merely

the punctuation at the end of a moment's
looking, a dot in a lifetime's

seemingly endless line of ellipses . . . .

Elegy

> *The word for moonlight is moonlight.*
> —Don DeLillo

Your phone number on the fridge

—your voice—or the baby teeth
boxed in your mother's closet.

Or the stack of letters you left

beside your mattress, half-
covered by your blanket.

Or your blanket. I hold it up
for those who didn't know you,

expecting a movie to project there—.

How inadequate this is (I thought

perhaps the paper could be made
from your ashes). Still, something

must be said to land you in words

we learned together in childhood.
Something must be said

of the basement's stairlight,
the sloped street channeling us

it seemed into ourselves. Yes,

something must be said of plunging
blood-lipped into the surf,

or crossing the Boston snowcrust
whiskey-steamed, or jumping

into the strip mine—the anthracite
staining our clothes as though

we'd learned something.

And I need to tell you, first writer

I knew, that now I can't
understand what I've learned,

except figuratively.

And why that isn't enough.

Rounding the Corner into "Early Sunday Morning"

1.
The sunlight comes as if through a phonograph needle—
a robust chord of light that's somehow thin at the heart
of how it says what it has to say. Still, the walls
are soothed, long shadows stretching westward
from the hanging signs and the squat fireplug,
not-quite-vestigial tails of the street's unnamed life.

2.
As if the street has slipped underwater, has submerged
into the heavy stillness of a Sunday,—blurred names
in the shop windows, returned to the empty shapes they were
before they married the people and spaces I've come to know.
A hairdryer roars faintly back in a second floor window,
the sound framed by that window, as in my mind
I frame the image of a woman blow-drying her hair.

3.
The street as a cavernous room, a concert hall defined
by blue walls that come down just beyond the rooftops.
And rounding the next corner, I'll enter the same room as this
with different furniture, although the decor, of course
will be similar. There will be names framed in the windows
of another law office, a pharmacy, or a closed barber shop
with its pole that's turned all night, winding up
the thread of all that names fail to say.

My Apartment As a Diorama

Of course, there are the necessary props—

straightback chairs, a walnut table,
but my favorite part's the cityscape

through the window, so detailed
despite tiny scale—a scaffolding

framing the hospital doorway,
pedestrians entering on crutches,

ceasing to be pedestrians
when the doors slide shut behind them.

The apartment windows indicate
a city of the smallest narratives—

lit caves in which people keep
discovering fire for the first time.

On the street below, a bag lady
pushing her shopping cart

and an ambulance
pushing its dim headlights—

so near the emergency room;
in here though, it will never arrive

to unload its merchandise.
Sometimes the mouth of the world

opens—though at the last minute,
it always holds its tongue.

Cohesion Triptych

———Looking out the Window

on a late-January evening, wind
joined to one side of the glass,

my breath to the other. Jeanne's
washing dishes, the radio

pressing notes through tin
(the street rattling a muffler).

And now she's singing along
to the lyrics' prescription,———

pills forming in her mouth.
All these shared words,

or borrowed (they're never
really *ours,* if they were

we couldn't speak). Words
hanging like sacked marbles.

Each night, we voice-flick
for the glass roll, our souls

like colors there inside them,
while outside, under the snow,

the fallen leaves are frozen
in the same sheet of ice———

——Snow

Winter painting was an indoor activity
until the invention of disposable tubes.
Once the oils could go with them,
painters ventured out into nature
to improvise snowscapes—the canvas
joining the blank,

fallen world. Snow's logic:
reflection *and* absorption—
shadows under the surface,
snowbanks somehow radiating
the sky. Flakes hit the salted
street like unrecorded notes

while cars score lines in the wet—.
Soon slush fills the gutters,—
some dark tainting the palette,
and why shouldn't it stay?
The world's been quieted,
like an apartment after lunch—

sound overwhelmed and pinned
to the ground—. I'm undeniably
present, here at the bus stop
breathing my own warmth
against my hands. While the flakes
keep disappearing into my face.

——New Year's Eve, Cape Cod

Black water—flat and in motion.
Stars—holes where the canvas

is coming apart. Air so cold,
it's substanceless, my breath

spongy against it. Pinpricks
of speech from up at the house,

where a tent looms, Antarctic
in the front yard, though

no music yet—everything's
in the process of setting up.

Thus, I'm poised to enter
the party's anonymity (which is

of course a perpetual state).
Still, there's something

to be said for being here—
deep-pocketed by the night's

strange place, joined
to all that's larger than me,

though in me in a sense—.
And there's the promise

of words that will come
as each song fails to persevere—

Ice Storm

The neighborhood sealed shut as in memory.
A tree fell against the light pole
which in turn fell across the yard—

split heartwood glossed with ice,
young leaves like shriveled hands
wearing glass gloves. Down the street

basketball hoops hang like chandeliers,
saplings have been dipped in clear wax,
cars are nailed fast to their driveways

with crystalline spikes. Cataracts
on house windows through which
the neighborhood can be half-seen.

An old woman on the couch
beside the grand piano
exposing its intricate tendons,

the clear stillness happening,
cordoning her in that hollow space—
her basket of broken glasses.

Empty Warehouse

Its mere emptiness invites imagination,
which, invited, enters. This interior
could hold a house

(as a body can hold a life, or a life
can hold belief). Though here,
it's all been stripped away—

even the memories must be projected
from remembered pictures—
machines stamping, filing cabinets

with their papers like tree rings,
and the hovering faith in a paycheck
reified in the production

of that paycheck. The windows
are time-lacquered with dust, the lights
unable to buzz into light.

Imagine the timeclock's hands
still in motion—not frozen
beneath the cracked glass—,

imagine them crossing each other,
entangling the hours to be stored away
like yarn, as the hours

with or without record
entangle us. Nothing's here
but the possibility emptiness provides.

In a far corner,
a door that won't quite shut allows
a bookspine of world—

Dear Sappho,

I know my body's a placeholder for light,
and still I breathe into it as heat

breathes into the mouth of a sailing balloon.
I find I'm moving away from myself

and further into myself—each second
thought slips through the body like music

through the wood of a violin. In Vermont,
I once wrote my name in the snow

dusting the ice on a lake, though now
it's as if the ink has left the paper and gone

back into the pen. And just this hour,
my hands have grown colder—evidence

that the body keeps evolving into itself,
while a snowscape is so complete

all that remains for it is to fade—
a retreat to beginning. Though retreat

is also a kind of arrival, just as wind
means someplace else is emptying—or

driving at night, I keep choosing the space
lit up by my headlights. And sleep?—

sleep is poor proof of an emptiness
inside us—sleep turns the body into world.

Yet, sometimes I'm stunned by the light
of the fridge when I finally open my eyes;

other times my apartment is vast
and hollow as a dream. You wrote about

touching the sky with both arms,
but that was clearly meant as a metaphor—

the airplane in which I came here
rested on the intricate web of city lights

reflected in the underside of its wings.
Perhaps I mean that when the body falls,

the mind rises like a floor to meet it,
or perhaps that standing on the ice

was like standing on the finger of God.
Neighbors' voices blend in a courtyard

like smoke from as many chimneys
rising toward what?—surely not

a sky we can touch. And though
we can't touch what's beyond a window,

we can touch the window and pretend
it's a photograph. I can rest my hand

on this letter as I write it, and numbly
feel the recipient's skin. My lover's

thoughts are the charge in a pale cloud
I want to land on, like settling down

in one of those thinly imagined
rectory paintings of heaven. I know

how these bodies carry us down
the long hallway toward the kitchen

or the bed, pleasure planted inside them
like flight in the wings of a bird.

But love requires opening
the impossible inside us, and even then,

the mind keeps trying to arrive
at the other side of *here*.

Sunset Study

Then daylight drains through night's fine sieve;
what's floated there all afternoon

gets caught by the wire mesh,—
bulbs across bridges, windows in the skyline,

the blistering moon. Sluice of orange
across the bay, taillights on the entrance ramp—.

A stony gray has been rolling westward
since Sisyphus clocked out at five,

still dressed for the day there in his window,
frying potatoes on a half-sized stove.

Cars passing on the highway—
belted songs, arguments with the rear-view mirror—

seconds muted by thick glass.
And the barbecuers talking on their roofs,

sipping beers, walking up to the edge cautiously,
like runners to a starting line—.

Under the street, commuters hold the handpoles
anchored to the train's motion;

as bridges sway with the breeze, the calendar
is endlessly eastwardly turning.

And now a cab driver logs another fare,
a cop another arrest—

our written history, these lists of tangencies.
Each time the wind dies

we're left alone with our breath.
A boy begins practicing trumpet on the first floor—

THREE

Because the Water

                   held me in its surface
before I entered it. And beneath the cupola
I was a blood drop in an egg.

You told me Epicurus believed
the sun was only as large as it appeared
but he was wrong. In the alley

behind the discoteque, all I did to get in
was press my hand against a stranger's hand.
The spices on the Cours Saleya

made richer pigments than pigments,
the umbrellas poured their coaled light
all afternoon. And at night

the rails shifted like a sleeper's twitch,
so the whole train changed direction.
I could see the museum's plate glass window

from my window, I watched the sky reflect
the water there. When I entered you
you held me in your surface, as my hand

absorbed the surface of your sound.
The snow stretched from the cabin window
like a drying sail—

I know foolishly that it was made
of water. The tapered tip of each branch
is the exposing of its center

according to DaVinci, and the knives
in the kitchen smelled inextricably of onions.
(On the rocks, your mouth tasted of onions.)

The butcher flirted with his eyes
as he halved chickens against a board,
we agreed the cross was like a bull's-eye

through the open doorway. And then
the wall pressed back when I pinned
you to it, and the words from the speaker

were spoken in notes. The words
from the speaker were spoken with meaning.
The wine we swiped from the cabinet

was nearly vinegar, but the terrace
was warm and pale and the honey
held in its fabric a trace of the field.—

The bees too must have tasted of lavender.

Night Stop, South of Lyon

The dull gray crisscross
of moonlit tracks, orange-pith
fluorescence filling the station.
A technicality (no one got on)—

just enough pause
for the platform to enter
(and anchor) me. By the time
I noticed the dark

town up on the hill—buildings
(I like to think) like sealed geodes—
the cars began again
negotiating their team inertia.

My five (second class) companions
breathed their dreams
into the atmosphere

of our compartment,
(becoming the atmosphere)
as the world turned back
to passing air. Motion

skylessly suspended us
in our dark (ticking) box.
Only when the first wet light
began to fill the smear

did I find myself again in context.
My position was one of faithful
servitude—(I tried to guess
the time by that new light).

Four Atget Photographs

1. Rue de Nevers

The sudden open that breathes it in:
the stucco walls shedding their skin,
the wet street and light holding fast
to each other (and collodion—
its chemical hug like mother-of-pearl).
The camera fixed here in the street,
the street in the camera. Windows part-
covered by jalousie shutters, the sky
flat-white and blinding. Listen:

the light's sincere in its silence—

2. Passage Vandrezanne

The long dim alley telescoped shut—
flat now, though I can see deep into it,
up the cobbled, wafer-thin steps
to an opening in the distance: a street
fastened board-like across its path.
No doorways here, just one fixed
destination—the walls that channel us,
steep and blank, their light revealed
through long development. Let's say

it was dark, made light by looking—

3. Asphalters

Light like oil on the still-wet surface—
matte-glare and empty; three men
team-weaving it, like weaving a river.
Lying where it is, the placement
seems haphazard—sand beneath,
wood-strips holding the edges,
ending beyond the lip. Their floats
continue divining level, and kneeling
they're endlessly backing away

from their work, which hardens—

4. Nymphéa

Lotuses caught in mid-explosion—
petals like frozen insect wings,
anthers redacted by pollen. Stems
rise muscularly from the water
(slipping through gravity's net),
mirror-split from their reflections,
which rise and fall as the sun
puppets around the flower-faces.
Broad leaves like elephant ear

launchpads, fixed in their floating—

Pollock

See the man crossing the stubble field,
cutting a swath through the falling

light of the afternoon. See how his shadow
covers the shadow-pegs—all brushed

to the northeast—until a cloud washes over.
Now watch the trees in their papery

caress of the sky, or the gaping barn
light-speared through the slats,

or the farmhouse holding its stillness
against the gate's squeaking hinge

(shadows inside them like water
in the hulls of ships). Then the shadows

are released from the cloud's erasure,
so they return to fall over and over

into their illusions of continuum.
Watch the paint threading down

from his brush—as if in the distance
of its fall it could have landed

anywhere. But then it fell
into its space on the canvas, just

as each shadow falls into itself,
just as the man falls

into himself each second—

Vermont

He leaves on his impressions of the snow
a hint of eyelashes.

The car leaves in the snow's falling body
a breath of shape.
                              Around him,
shut houses in a face of fields,

buried stone walls he must remember
into being.

                    Yesterday's cold East River
is extant and unbreathable—

dark air in a forever
snow-sealed barn. The passing trees

will hold their breath
for months, beneath the snow's light,

the fields grip tight their frozen furrows.

The tires push against the slush-
slicked lines of asphalt to generate

a house, the radio, the mirror light
his memory of her   **69**

reads by. All-he's-done
is, but he knows no longer touches him.

The world's impenetrable beauty keeps
billowing around itself

like some Great Northern Jellyfish.
He belongs, in that

he's endlessly folding back in—

Dear Sappho,

Everything's always in focus at once,
except to the living. That's why

it's so beautiful here this evening—
the trees' skinless ribs beneath a sky

flattened with clouds. And now
my neighbor hammering his roof

into the cold night, and now passing
cars like hollowed-out shadows.

In the gas station, a flier rain-stuck
to the windshield of a blue

pickup—; and now music
filling the rooms like snow in a field,

and sometimes lyrics emerge
through the melting. Once I lived

miles from here, on a street I try
to hang in the window. How my breath

nails down my footsteps, how my eyes
pull the light through each slide—.

So tonight I'll fill the bathtub
with water, the bathroom with steam—

I'll only bury my body where I'm able
to see it. Always your breath

is a trace in the air—just a thread
of your unraveled view. And now

yours is the dark street
I begin to wake into—like the street

below this room: all the windows
lit up with curtains.

From the Porch

We breathe light.

—James Wright

So what's at issue is light—
our tangling with its silent mythology.

Or what's at issue are shadows—
hiding behind the railing's rungs
as we hide from the sun
like siblings beneath the house's skirt.

What's at issue is air—
words gripping its thick wet fur
while it fills us and leaves us.

Or maybe it's movement—
slipping by in a whisper,
the bay's blue exhaling its luster
as light and time continue their gossip,
Earth endlessly turning away.

Or rhythm—
descending undulations of steps
meeting the endless arrival of waves,
the countless little squares
in the screens, windows of days.

Perhaps what's at issue is surfaces—
planar joints, the walls of the house
sponging up light, the water
rising now in a darkening tide,
creeping up the sandbar
like a hand on a thigh.

Or what's between us—
slack lines knotted too far back
within us to feel; each second
your face in a different light
as a white sail edges across the bay.

The Poem in Which We're Stieglitz and O'Keeffe

When I photograph I make love.
—Stieglitz

You're shadow and light,
a composition of tonalities.

A swath of dark across
the copper of your shoulder,

or the white of your tank-top—
though beneath it

you're veiled in shadows.
From ten feet away

I'm holding you in my hands,
and of course

the goal of this is to capture,
if only for a second.

When you breathe
you breathe into my eye—

a second's enough,
here's the image that lasts.

Suspension Triptych

——*The Blind Swimmer*

The water's seal around her body—
so that each stroke

locates her. She's alone
with her joints' dull creaks, the water

slipping past, the sound
of air through the space she makes.

The lifeguard watches
from the side, holding his breath

as she approaches each wall—
Like catching the horizon, like waking

into an answer, so she can plant
and push back off . . . .

——Waiting for the Train

By the 9th Street stop,
he's waiting in his car
for his lover to return from the city.

He reads the paper, watches commuters
through the stillness of the glass.
The street's an infirmary

of inanimate amputees:
an unhinged door against a wall,
a hairbrush stuck in the street's hot tar,

a busted tire by the stop sign,
and all the plucked feathers of garbage
swirling through traffic—

flattened soda cans, newspaper pages,
fliers for sidewalk sales.
Each second she's getting closer,

floating on the metal tracks,
for the first time in a week
looking forward to him.

The fight about whatever-it-was
finally broke like a fever,
so now she slips into listening

to the stranger beside her
as he talks in his sleep.

——Unsendable Letters

It's too dark for her to see what she's writing.
Lying back on the couch,
she's joined the glass coffee table

and the prints of paintings
in their invisibility. The boy's tucked into bed,
perhaps four in the morning,

and she's alone with the pen's felt tip
floating on the surface of the paper.
Outside, the newspaper's already on the stoop,

an unexpected drizzle
printing a ghost of the front page
onto the pale concrete. So much was never said—

now the words can finally leave her.
She gives them back
the way a swimmer sweats into the water.

The Problem of Landing

Light smoothed across us, across the bed,
into the fields—light with the corners
tucked in beyond the trees.

Flecks of news rise off the fire—
blown back to the air—disembodied time?
Take the small fist of a letter,

poke at it, open its hand,
change the word. How do we project?—
like the air in a flame. And trains

slip past deserted rooms,
the water tower fills and empties—
long-unappreciated lung. Notice the cross

on the window's open heart,
and oh, how soon the tomatoes are reddening.
Out in the fields, there's nothing

but light—I found my way home
by its endless projection. If my past is flight
and my present is landing,

I must never quite touch the ground,
and how can this be? The street
like a long blank tape, passing carlights

through the car's glass skin.
Not all surface, not all substance—
clouds drifting through a pale blue sky

in the shop windows on Main Street,
or see how the cornstalk tips
make a ground above the ground—

Double Aubade

This page (whether read or burned) is lit
by the world; now across the street
the deli begins to fill, and the sun

still blocked by a crisscross of branches.
A day takes shape by dissolving itself—
the light erasing itself, the light

erasing itself—. Though clapping
gathered to a room of applause, the lights
rose to sort us to our cars, the ride home

a thin reeling into sleep. And now
the coffee's black as the hole in the guitar,
blank undersides of leaves

pale with sky, the roof's imbricate design
hovers up there like a wing. I keep
falling through the window

of my body, the radio painting me,
my gaze narrowed to a book—its words
I must cross to repeat. I can't stop

the notes from sliding into each sentence
as it collapses back into the page.
And I'm not sad

when the light changes its skin,
when someone disappears around a corner
again, when each word must end.

2.

O night
          withdrawn to the drawers,
the closets, the hard spaces

of objects:
          inkfill the letters,
bury yourself in blue. And day,

hold on
          to the tip of my finger,
let your dawn breathe against me

like the explosion
          of an airbag. O day,
raise your billboards, façades,

land your light
          on my skin like sand,
land your feet on the flypaper

of photographs.
          Dear photographs,
burned filaments, show me my eyes

last week,
          my hand in her hair.
Rest in the desk beside the bed,

I'll open
          its window onto you—.
And words, how I reach for you,

and blindly
        through you. Please
speak to me now, as you disappear,

so often
        and hopelessly
I've longed to be loved by you.

The Undressing

See the roofs from the deck,
see these hands on the railing.

Branches cut the wind like rudders,
though nothing is steered.

Oh, this steering is nothing—
each second like a leaf in water,

losing its color. Once a firefly
floating in a wine glass,

once a pool-lit cocktail party.
Once a moth's ash wings

pinned between my fingers.
Once down the backyard hill—,

once sunspots faded on my skin
where she touched me once.

Once footprints in the snow
I stepped in each day to class,

once water sopping the sheet
beneath the porch door.

I went on vacation once—
there were open shells

on the kitchen table.
Once the garage was clean,

I parked the car in there.
After dinner once

she opened her shirt to me,
and just as each image

opens inward on another image,
I hold inside me

her sleeping body
like a patch of dandelions,

waiting for the wind.

Notes/Sources

Opening epigraphs: Morandi: quoted in *How You Look at It: Photographs of the 20th Century*; Bishop: "At the Fishhouses," *The Complete Poems, 1927-1979.*

"Self-Portrait in a Blank Room": Bill Viola, *Reasons for Knocking at an Empty House: Writings 1973-1994.*

"Reading Sonnevi on a Tuesday Night": Göran Sonnevi, *Mozart's Third Brain*, trans. Rika Lesser. (Thanks to Adam Zagajewski for the manuscript copy, since the book has not yet been published in English.)

"Ukrainian Egg": Epigraph from Milan Kundera, *Testaments Betrayed*, trans. Linda Asher.

"All the Ghosts Are Blind": The poem's opening assertion is more or less lifted from *The Notebooks of Leonardo Da Vinci*, trans. Edward MacCurdy.

"Trakl the Pharmacist": The poem is something of a "half-cento" in part cobbled from various poems by Georg Trakl, trans. Daniel Simko.

"Brodsky Smoking": Joseph Brodsky, *Watermark.*

"Cohesion Triptych: Snow": The opening "quote" is apocryphal, though the gist of it is, as far as I know, true.

"Elegy": Epigraph from Don DeLillo, *The Body Artist.* The poem is for Travis (Tip) Rushing (1976-2001).

"From the Porch": Epigraph from James Wright, "Yes, But," *Above the River.*

photo by Jeanne Ouellette

Wayne Miller was born in Cincinnati, Ohio, studied at Oberlin
College, and after working briefly in the Manhattan District
Attorney's Office, received an MFA from the University of
Houston. He is the author of a chapbook, *What Night Says to
the Empty Boat (Notes for a Film in Verse)*, and the recipient of a
Ruth Lilly Fellowship from the Poetry Foundation, the Lucille
Medwick Memorial Award from the Poetry Society of America,
and *Poetry* magazine's Bess Hokin Prize. His poems have
appeared in *Boulevard, Chelsea, Crazyhorse, Epoch, FIELD, The
Gettysburg Review, Hotel Amerika, LIT, The Paris Review, Poetry,
Quarterly West, Sycamore Review,* and on *Poetry Daily*. He lives in
Kansas City and teaches at Central Missouri State University,
where he co-edits *Pleiades: A Journal of New Writing*.

New Issues Poetry

David Dodd Lee, *Abrupt Rural; Downsides of Fish Culture*
M.L. Liebler, *The Moon a Box*
Alexander Long, *Vigil*
Deanne Lundin, *The Ginseng Hunter's Notebook*
Barbara Maloutas, *In a Combination of Practices*
Joy Manesiotis, *They Sing to Her Bones*
Sarah Mangold, *Household Mechanics*
Gail Martin, *The Hourglass Heart*
David Marlatt, *A Hog Slaughtering Woman*
Louise Mathias, *Lark Apprentice*
Gretchen Mattox, *Buddha Box; Goodnight Architecture*
Lydia Melvin, *South of Here*
Carrie McGath, *Small Murders*
Paula McLain, *Less of Her; Stumble, Gorgeous*
Sarah Messer, *Bandit Letters*
Wayne Miller, *Only the Senses Sleep*
Malena Mörling, *Ocean Avenue*
Julie Moulds, *The Woman with a Cubed Head*
Marsha de la O, *Black Hope*
C. Mikal Oness, *Water Becomes Bone*
Bradley Paul, *The Obvious*
Katie Peterson, *This One Tree*
Elizabeth Powell, *The Republic of Self*
Margaret Rabb, *Granite Dives*
Rebecca Reynolds, *Daughter of the Hangnail; The Bovine Two-Step*
Martha Rhodes, *Perfect Disappearance*
Beth Roberts, *Brief Moral History in Blue*
John Rybicki, *Traveling at High Speeds* (expanded second edition)
Mary Ann Samyn, *Inside the Yellow Dress; Purr*
Ever Saskya, *The Porch is a Journey Different From the House*
Mark Scott, *Tactile Values*
Hugh Seidman, *Somebody Stand Up and Sing*
Martha Serpas, *Côte Blanche*
Diane Seuss-Brakeman, *It Blows You Hollow*
Elaine Sexton, *Sleuth*
Marc Sheehan, *Greatest Hits*

Heidi Lynn Staples, *Guess Can Gallop*
Phillip Sterling, *Mutual Shores*
Angela Sorby, *Distance Learning*
Matthew Thorburn, *Subject to Change*
Russell Thorburn, *Approximate Desire*
Rodney Torreson, *A Breathable Light*
Robert VanderMolen, *Breath*
Martin Walls, *Small Human Detail in Care of National Trust*
Patricia Jabbeh Wesley, *Before the Palm Could Bloom: Poems of Africa*